T0171718

What your Momma never told you about the day you were born

NIKKI KRAUS

BALBOA.PRESS

A DIVISION OF HAY HOUSE

Balboa Press books may be ordered through booksellers or by contacting:

Balboa Press
A Division of Hay House
1663 Liberty Drive
Bloomington, IN 47403
www.balboapress.com
844-682-1282

Print information available on the last page.

ISBN: 979-8-7652-3199-9 (sc)
ISBN: 979-8-7652-3200-2 (e)

Balboa Press rev. date: 07/29/2022

What your momma never told you about the day you were born

by Nikki Kraus

A special message to you...

Sweet Libra.

This book is all yours.

Color it up.

Add your name.

Make it yours.

On the day
you
were born...

every star

+

every planet

+

everything...

...was in the
perfect place
for you
to arrive.

From The Creator
above and through
a magical circle
of animals
called
The Zodiac...

you were born

You came into
this beautiful world
at the most perfect
moment

And you are a Libra!

A set of scales is your
fun little symbol in
the Zodiac

Balance is a
big deal
for you just like a
scale system.

But most
importantly,
you are one of the
brightest stars
in the whole wide
world.

Like a beautiful
butterfly,
you float through
this world on the
very air you were
made from.

That air up in
the sky brings
you to life...

because you are
air.

In that big sky
up there,
one planet is
all yours.

It's called Venus.

This planet
fills your
personality
with love
a desire
for beauty.

All the pretty
things are
your favorite
and this
makes you
a natural artist.

Charm:
it is your
gift to the world.

This means other
people love you
because you just know
how to make them
smile and laugh.

On your journey
here on Earth,
approval and love
from others
is key to your
happiness.

Pssst! It is ok to say no

All that yummy
energy you
have...
comes from
your friends.

Being alone can
make you sad.

You listen.

You feel.

You let others
just be
themselves.

On your many
adventures,
a partner is very
important.

Always take a
friend along.

A strong team player, you are!

And you will win all the games in life because you know how to pick the best teammates

Peace.
It's your goal in life

(((and sometimes you
ignore your own feelings just
to make other people
happy)))

There is a
special rock for
you, Libra.

It is called an
opal.

She helps you with
money.

She helps you make
better decisions.

She frees you from big
feelings like greed
and jealousy.

Hiding behind that happy smile is a big and brilliant brain.

This brilliant brain helps you make new things (inventions are a strong move for you).

It helps you go fun places.

It helps you meet new people.

That big and open
mind of yours loves to
see and think about
this world around
you.

Create all the
beautiful things,
Libra!

People are your
favorite playground,
Libra.

Go to every sleepover.

Make all the new
friends.

But never forget to
stand up for yourself,
Libra.

Because you matter.

Go to every sleepover.

Make all the new
friends.

But never forget to
stand up for yourself,
Libra.

Because you matter.

Remember

You are a bright and shining star in this world.

People love to be around you because you make them feel so special.

Trust yourself.

You have really
great thoughts
and
strong ideas.

When you notice sad
faces or others being
treated poorly, you
shine even brighter.

Courage to stick up
for others is your
super-strength!

This world is a happy place for you and big hugs make it even happier.

Play is your work.

Work is your play.

Do all the things,
Libra.

Just keep moving!

Play.

Fly.

Be that happy star
we all love so
much.

Live like a butterfly
floating through the
wildflowers, you will
meet many new friends
in your life.

They love you the
moment they meet you.

Always.

Always.

Always.

Trust Yourself,
Libra.

Because you are
absolutely perfect!

You are much more than just
your sun sign, Libra.

Exploring and discovering your
entire birth chart is a brilliant
way to understand yourself more
deeply.

This can be done online and with
the help of someone like me.

Feel free to reach out to me in
any way for more discovery about
yourself and who you really are.

Nikki Kraus

541-604-0595

theenikkikraus@gmail.com

Printed in the United States
by Baker & Taylor Publisher Services